# Erha

## Volume 4
## Loving Leland

Captioning, Design, Graphics and
Layout by David K Petersen

Black Creek Press
Ludington Michigan

Copyright 2004 All Rights Reserved ©
http://blackcreekpress.com

# Dedication

Loving Leland is dedicated to Edmund Peters.
I'd like to say thank you Edmund for sharing your families history.
Without your invaluable help this volume of Loving Leland would
have been much less.

# Foreword

I'm very pleased to be able to present this book of images from the Erhardt Peters collection for your enjoyment.

Many Leland people are familiar with some of Erhardt's photographic works. He sold many photographs in the Leland area and some are available to be viewed by the public at the Bluebird Restaurant, and now the Leelanau Museum in Leland.

It is my hope that in sharing these photographs I am able to take the reader on an eclectic visual journey to Leland's past. I am not a native of Leland, nor do I have any history there. I was however taken in by the artistic beauty of the Leland photographs, the talent behind the lens that created them, and the desire to preserve and share as many as I could.

About 400 images are included in each volume and while some views may be familiar many more are sure to be new and previously unpublished.
In my discussions with Erhardt's children and other family members, it is obvious that his heart was always in Leland, and Erhardt's passion is reflected in his views of the places and people he held close.

This is the first of three volumes of a series of books about Leland. Loving Leland is the the first of the Leland books, but is #4 in the series of Erhardt Peters pictorials. Once the 3 volumes are complete it is my hope to combine the best 1000 images from a half dozen collections into one hard cover volume with color and additional graphics.

I'm also going to take this opportunity to get on my soapbox. There are many wonderful images and historically important artifacts stored away in shoeboxes, attics and basements. These things need to be protected, preserved and shared.

Many of Erhardt's prints and negatives were destroyed in the fire and many more lost when his son's building collapsed and was razed. Finally the collection was dispersed through an estate sale, auction and the remainder liquidated in a private sale to collectors. Please take a few moments to reflect on how you might share and preserve your families treasures.

# The Peters Family History in Leland

## John Peters Family at the Leland home August 1922

Authors note: I think it is important for several reasons to provide the reader with some background on Erhardt Peters and his pioneer family to illustrate the forces of man and nature that shaped and influenced the photographic works presented in this volume.

Many thanks to the Peters family for providing the biographical, family history, and interviews that allowed me to assemble this section.

Erhardt's grandfather Johann Peters born February 25th 1839 in Gropel, Hanover Germany arrived in Leland in the early 1860's. He had left his home for America because his parents had made an arranged marriage with the Millers daughter and he did not wish to marry her.

After coming to America he came to Michigan and went to work in the woods near East Leland. It was while working there that he became seriously injured and came to depend on the care of Adelaide Steffens [born February 2nd 1847 in Eversdorf Hanover Germany] It was during this time while he recovered, as it so often happens, they fell in Love.

Johann and Adelaide married November 11th 1866 and moved into Good Harbor where they lived for several years.

John Peters was born in 1866 at Good Harbor on Good Harbor Bay. [Now a part of the Sleeping Bear NationalPark]

At that time Good Harbor was becoming a bustling little community.

Ironically in 1924 John would purchase the salvage rights to the village of Good Harbor and dismantle the town building by building as Erhardt documented the last breath of this tiny village with his camera.

The photos are reputed to be the only surviving images of the buildings that made up the village of Good Harbor.

Some of the materials were used in buildings still standing today such as what used to be the Nicholas hotel on the hill, as well as the garage at the Peters home.

Johann became employed by the Leland Iron Company as an engineer a few years later. He was paid $1.25 for a 12 hour days work at the Foundry. Later his son John Peters would on occasion recall the flames shooting out of the cupola at night and that the charcoal smoke was so thick that women covered the faces of their babies when out of doors.

As a young boy John would play around the furnace and run errands for the men working there and watch tugboats like the August Julius tow a big scow up Lake Leelanau , returning with buggies full of charcoal on the deck from the charcoal kilns and camps up the lake.

On May 2nd of 1876 Johann's wife Adelaide died in childbirth, and Johann stricken with grief over the loss of his wife and unable to care for himself or his children took his own life leaving John and his 3 siblings to the care of relatives. John lived with his uncle George Kahrs and remained at home to work on the farm while his cousins attended school. John's formal education ended at the fourth grade.

He would on occasion talk about life on the farm and how he would awaken in his upstairs loft to find that snow had drifted in through the cracks in the walls and that his hair was frozen to the pillow.

John Peters and his brother Dick worked for their Uncle Dick Steffens and at other farms and in the lumber camps as young adults.

Johann and Adelaide had 4 children, John, sitting, Dick standing, Anna standing and Vena sitting to John's right.

Dick was a farmer in the Leland area, Anna born December 5th 1870 married Gustave Wakulet. Vena born June 17th 1873, married George Olson.

The above photograph is of the lifesaving crew circa 1886 from North Manitou Island where a very young John Peters is shown [back row far left] . His duties with the crew are at this time unknown but it shows that there may have been an early interest in a Maritime Life that would eventually become his career.

Left to right John Peters Unknown in center Merlin Brown on the end, sitting Alec Macon and Oswald Carder Sr.

John worked several years for John Porter who had come to the Leland area as a Government Agent and teacher to the Indians at Old Mission and later when Porter moved to Omena on Grand Traverse Bay.

In the 1890's when work was scarce due to a financial panic John walked to Empire during the winter and from there to Honor where he worked in a lumber camp for 15.00 a month and board. During a subsequent winter John walked to Northport and then across Grand Traverse Bay to Eastport in order to find work for two winters in a lumber camp near East Jordan that was owned by his former employer John Porter.

After his early years of working in lumber mills and having acquired experience in the woods he spent a considerable time working for the Lime Lake Lumber Company, & Schomberg Brothers at Good Harbor buying logs for Culver at Cedar and cruising timber on South Manitou Island.

John was married on May 18[th,] 1898 to Anna Fitschen at her home in Good Harbor. John and Anna had six children. The first was born at the farm in Good Harbor, now part of Sugar Loaf Estates near where the Manitou market is located.

The remaining five children were born in Leland at the home they purchased for 600.00 in 1899.

Stella was the oldest child and born in Good Harbor Arnold, Ewald, Erhardt, Wilfred, to the right, and Edmund pictured below at age 6.

Stella born March 19th 1899 married Oswald Meltzer and then George Fritz. She was a teacher in a one room school in Gratiot County.

Arnold born June 13th 1901 married Myrtle Becker in 1927 and worked for Western Electric in Chicago.

Ewald born 1903 was injured in an accident and passed away in 1923 at age 20.

Erhardt born December 1904 married Alice Nelson in 1941

Wilfred born 1907 and passed away in 1935 due to complications from Tuberculosis. He worked at the Leland Enterprise for 10 years.

Edmund born May 29th 1909 married Bernice Garthe in 1934. He went to County Normal School in Northport Leelanau County, graduating from Northern Michigan College at Marquette. Edmund worked aboard the PM 21 in the Galley and also on the Lightship tender Sumac.

He taught for 40 years at several schools including Good Harbor, Glen Haven, Suttons Bay, Traverse City, Manitou Island, and Bloomfield Hills.

John entered the mill business again, first in a mill located on the north bank, a short distance down from lake Leelanau, later a sawmill which burned to the ground May 26th 1892. 500,000 board feet of lumber was lost, $1,500.00 in value and no insurance.

Later John Peters owned a shingle mill directly across the river from the courthouse where Erhardt would say they used to go to watch the steam engine and governor as they puffed and whirled, laboring and speeding up as the saws went through the logs.

They would watch the shingle sawyers and weavers at work until the men chased them away from the machinery. John Peters had a Cedar Camp at the north end of Lake Leelanau with 2 or 3 employees. They would cut the cedar logs and raft them down the lake to the mill which was first located on the end of Cedar Street and then located at Mill Street.

In these mills John Peters was his own engineer. Once when working in the mill he was caught by a belt, whipped up to the shaft overhead, breaking his arm and dislocating his shoulder and otherwise painfully injured, but several days later he was back on the job, in the mill splinted and bandaged.

When the days of the sawmill in Leland were past, he dismantled the mill, sold the machinery and took what was offered to support his growing family of 6 children. During the next few years John Peters conducted his last logging operations in Good Harbor and for his brother on the Ribble place south of Leland. There were still new challenges and careers ahead for John that were yet to unfold.

Loading Logs for shipment at North Manitou by Beebe circa 1910

John Peters began working at Good Harbor for the Schomberg Brothers as a Dock Foreman supervising the loading crews. He continued working at North Manitou Island in 1909 as a dock foreman loading ships with lumber until he found work with John Versnyder as the Chief Engineer on the Steamer Leelanau for 5 summers from 1912 to 1916.

They would make the run to meet the train at Provemont and then to Perrin's landing at the south end of Lake Leelanau. The Ship it's schedule ran as long as the lake remained open.

In 1916 John Peters went to work for the Lighthouse service as the first assistant engineer on LV-56, the Lightship Manitou Shoals near where the Crib Lighthouse is located now.

John's service in the lighthouse service began at the time he was nearly 50 and young Erhardt was 10 years old.

John served on the Manitou Shoals Lightship, 11 Foot Shoal, Peshtigo Lightship on Green Bay, Gray's Reef, Milwaukee Lightship and the Huron.

John retired in 1937 shortly before the lighthouse service became part of the Coast Guard. When at age 70 he finally stepped off the Lightship Huron he had not set foot on land for 3 stormy months. John always said "We take what we get and we do the best we can", and he lived by that philosophy from the days of Oxens and schooners to when he passed away July 13th 1958 at the age of 92.

Pictured below is the last wooden Lightship serving in the Great Lakes. This ship LV-56 was stationed at White Shoals from 1891 to 1909 then North Manitou from 1910 to 1926. From there to Grays Reef from 1927 to 1928 and finally retired in December 1937 .

At that time John Peters had served the longest period of time on the Manitou. The ship was taken to Charlevoix to be dismantled.

The Milwaukee shown below is at the dock in Charlevoix Michigan in October of 1932. Once they left Charlevoix they were to head out to the east coast for re-assignment as a relief ship. They made port at Buffalo New York and wintered over in that port rather then to make for the coast as the ship had not been refitted for service in the Atlantic Ocean.

John Peters is seen below in the Manitou Lightship tender "tug" coming out of Leland's fishtown in August of 1922.
To the right is the Grays Reef Lightship

Below is the Lightship Manitou LV-89 anchored almost 7 miles out in Lake Michigan marking the shoal extending south east from North Manitou Island.

The ship was painted black which served to warn vessels that they should pass to the left, Red would indicate passing to the right.

This ship served from 1927 to 1933-34 then being replaced by LV-103 until 1934-35. For the next two years it served as a relief vessel until being decommissioned about 1936.

Erhardt Peters born December 10th 1904 to John and Anna Peters became interested in photography at a young age.

His first darkroom was in the basement of his parents home in Leland Michigan.

It was a small room and the only access in and out was a piece of white pine board 2 and ½ feet x 5 feet long swinging on a nail. In this tiny room he developed the film taken in his expeditions

Erhardt is decked out in what looks like his Sunday best. The men are loading ice blocks into the horse drawn sleds during the annual ice harvest. Below left Erhardt and crew are doing some winter canoeing and Charlie Kropp is working away at his forge in old Good Harbor.

Erhardt & Edmund above

Erhardt's love of Leland where he grew up is reflected in his many photos of the region's people, fishtown, and surrounding area.

He would travel by canoe up and down the Leelanau River and out to the islands with his Camera. Earlier he had a Eastman box camera and later a 2x3 Zeiss Ikon

Sometimes traveling alone and at times with maybe a friend or two, he took pictures as he traveled and captured the spirit and life of this small community on film.

Many photos captured daily life, series of photographs showing ice being cut on the lake in winter, cutting wood in the fall, and fishing aboard the tugs out of Leland's Fishtown.

He often set up series of photographs to show how something was done or to showcase a day in the life.

Left Fishermen mending nets at Fishtown.

Erhardt's family roots ran deep in Leland, also with maritime lore and life and this is reflected in his artistic photos of the great lakes, shipping and seamen. He enrolled at Central Normal School in Mount Pleasant and studied Geology there but did not pursue it.

Instead Erhardt began working on the Pere Marquette Car-ferries out of Ludington Michigan about January of 1927. He also spent time working in a bakery, a funeral home, sold fire alarms, was a night watchman, had a charter service in Leland, and was one of the main organizers for the Independent Car-ferry Union of the Great Lakes [1939-1941]

Below crew members aboard the Joshua A Hatfield pose for a photo.

Bottom the Pere Marquette 22 is seen outside the Ludington Harbor

Alice Peters parking for a photo on M-116 north of Ludington before driving the Carferry Workers Independent Union entry in the 4th of July parade circa 1941.

The Union was in existence from 1939 to 1941 before being absorbed into the Seafarer's Union.

Left Erhardt on the PM 22.

He built his darkroom, his own car from an old frame, and the fastest iceboat on Lake Leelanau, He tinkered and he collected many things, always bringing more and more home.

He could see the historic value in many things that people would put out to be left for the dump and he saved many locally significant items. He had a love for salvaging and on his many excursions found some unique treasures

One such example is the ships wheel from a schooner that he donated to the Museum in Leland, and the safe door to the first city hall in Ludington which I was able to purchase at the estate auction. Prior to his death he had begun to count his collection of books and once he reached 8,000 he quit counting.

His love for photography was very apparent and was an ongoing theme in his life up to 1941. By the time he began work on the car-ferries out of Ludington he was about 23 years old. He would go around the ship taking pictures from every angle and perspective he could find, sometimes hanging precariously in midair to catch just the right shot.

Erhardt took thousands of photographs of the Great Lakes and life on the ships that he was stationed on. From the car-ferries to the Joshua A Hatfield, other ore-boats, and his time in the Coast Guard he continued to snap pictures every chance he could.

While moving a sailboat in the Ludington area he was injured and almost lost his foot. While he was in Ludington recuperating he would take his crutches and go up and down the streets downtown to exercise.

It was during these expeditions that he met a girl and eventually made this young woman his wife in 1941 and within a few years had 3 sons, John, Leland, [Lee] and Alan. It was about this time that he gave up on his photography and very few photographs other then those of family appear after this time.

Erhardt made a decision not to be an absentee husband and father and did not return to maritime work. Instead he worked for Continental motors in Muskegon during the war and as an Ironworker afterwards until he suffered a stroke in the 1960's.

Erhardt perished in a fire in his home in 1989.
His legacy of photographs was almost lost as well. Many antiques, books, ephemera, photographs and negatives burned and were lost in the fire, and many more were lost a few years later after the roof of the building they were housed in collapsed and the building razed.

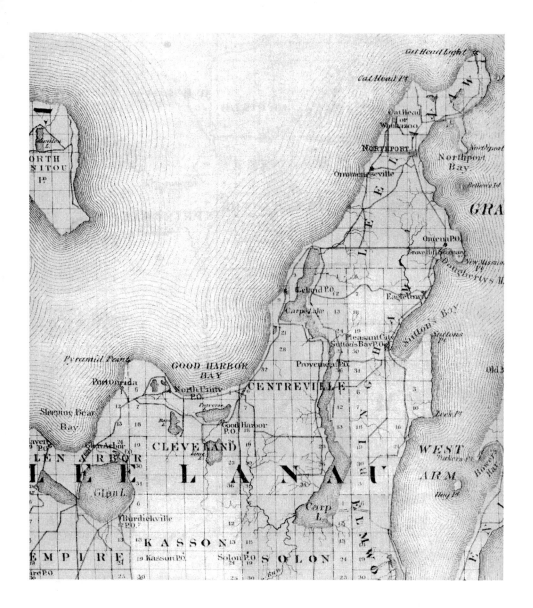

Above is a partial map of Leelanau County from Tackabury's 1873 County Atlas of Michigan.

I feel very fortunate to have been able to purchase these images. It is my personal goal to make the remaining extant photographs public so that they can be enjoyed and also that Erhardt Peters is finally able to be recognized for some of the great work that he did in capturing some extraordinary images. I am certain all who review this little book will enjoy them as much as I.

The Building of the Manitou at Leland Michigan. Big John Johnson never used power tools when building a boat. Above # EPLeland 223. Below Left James Anderson is caulking the Manitou. # EPLeland 224  Below Right Big John Johnson in front and James Anderson in back. # EPLeland 225.

John Johnson built the Manitou, Sambo and John A. Circa 1931.

#EPFM-004 Above Left
#EPFM-012 Above Right
#EPFM-023 Below Left EPleland-181

EPFM-032 Above EPFM-034 Below
I have captioned and identified as many of the locations, people, boats etc. as I can at this time. This book is meant to be a presentation of the photographic collections of Erhardt Peters rather then a history of the Leland area.

I would be happy to receive new information, corrections, or other interesting facts form the readers in order to make additions to future re-prints and the additional volumes.

The Manitou getting ready for the launch, Above EPFM-036

Below EPFM-035 Sliding into Leland Harbor, Big John is in the middle of the group.

EPfishtown-020 Launching of the Manitou

EPLeland 226 Below

EPLeland 227 Above

EPLeland 228 Left

The Manitou was used to deliver mail to North Manitou Island.

EPLeland 229


EPLeland 230

EPLeland 231
EPLeland 232
entering Leland
Harbor
EPLeland 233

A newly launched
North Manitou
coming into the
Leland Harbor.

EPFM-065 and EPFM-066

EPFT-103 This little ship called Manitou is shown beneath the power station that was closed in 1930. Tracy Grosvenor had a summer mailship and a winter mail ship, the Fern-L and the Manitou.

Using a smaller boat in the winter made it easier to pull it up on shore and to launch from the island during the stormy winter months.

Left to right: Oscar Holmstrom, Andrew Bourg, Charley Johnson, Alexander Holmstrom, Emil Bishop, Bill Anderson, Frank Johnson, Ernie Holmstrom. EPFT-106 Alexander Holmstrom is showing off the catch of the day.

Erhardt also collected and preserved photographs from in and around Leland that had been taken years earlier.

EPFT-112

EPFT-321

EPFT-118

EPFT-109 The Fern-L shown docked in Leland's Fishtown, nets drying on the right hand side of the photo.

EPFT-124

EPfishtown-052 Above

EPfishtown-055 Below Fish Nets are drying on the Docks while the Helen S on the left and the ACE is seen to the right.

EPFT-058 Above Ace of leland to the right and the ETTA coming into the river. **The Ace was owned by William Harting** with Otto Light as assistant during the 1928 season At the peak of the commercial fishing there were 8 rigs fishing out of the Leland harbor.

EPLeland-001 Looking south towards Whaleback.

EPLeland 234
 The **Fern-L was owned by Tracey Grosvenor.** Named after his daughter, the boat was a converted Coast Guard boat used to deliver mail to North Manitou Island. Tracey made daily runs during the summer season and attempted to make mail runs twice per week during the winter months.
EPLeland 235
Taking passengers to the island circa 1930.

EPLeland-236  In May of 1927 a 4 cylinder Hines marine engine was purchased from William Buckler and installed in the Fern-L

EPLeland 237

EPFT-127 The Nu Deal, Irene and 5 other fish tugs line the Leland Harbor.

EPFT-037 pictured below.

EPfishtown-004 Above left The **SAMBO** was owned by **George Cook**. The **Sambo was launched on August 18th 1926, and was built by John Johnson.**

EPFT-007

EPfishtown-010 Above The US Coast Guard Ship from North Manitou Island comes past the Violet as it enters the harbor at Leland.

EPfishtown-013 Below Carlson Brothers Fish tug Lucille coming into Leland Harbor with the days catch. Owned by the Carlson Brothers William, Gordon and Edwin. The Lucille was wrecked November 9th 1926 while at anchor at North Manitou. It was first thought to have broken loose and set adrift but a search proved futile and upon inspection it was found that the boat was sunk at the dock at the end of her anchor. It was raised 2 days later.

EPfishtown-022 Above The North Manitou

EPfishtown-034 below Note the spelling of Dimond. After it was pointed out that the spelling was not correct an A was added. Helen S to the left

EPfishtown-025 Above

EPLeland-004 Above

EPleland-010 Right two young boys take a pose for the camera.

EPfishtown-061 Above The Ace, Helen S and Diamond

EPfishtown-079 Below The Manitou is against the opposite shore, two young boys watch the water flow through the power company generator as the Etta lists slightly on the North bank.

EPfishtown-076 Above

EPfishtown-067 Below a 2 masted yacht J488 outside Leland Harbor circa 1930.

EPfishtown-100 Above

Below a very quiet fishtown wrapped in winter.

EPleland-031

Once the ice fields were moved out and the harbor opened the fishermen would often go out to set nets as early as possible in the season. They risked damage to the nets but after a couple months off the lakes many were eager to get back out as soon as possible.

EPfishtown-016 Above Fish Tugs Nu-Deal and Irene along with 2 others. At times the ice between Leland and Manitou Island would fill the lake and harbor blocking passage of the mail and raising havoc with the fishing boats as they attempted to get out early in the year to set their nets.

An easterly wind might carry off the ice one night and a shifting wind from the northwest could carry miles of ice fields into the bay, blocking the harbor and preventing the fishing fleet from reaching their nets the next. While the fish did not spoil during these early spring days the nets would sustain damage if the fishermen were unable to return to pull them .

EPfishtown-019 Above Fishing boats were generally pulled out of the water for the winter at the end of December each year. There were some occasions when the weather was unseasonably warm and the harbor remained open into January where they could continue to put out their nets. The catch was not generally as good but those fishermen who went out felt that they were at least able to harvest some small catches that would have gone uncaught otherwise.

EPfishtown-031 below

EPFT-121


EPleland-091

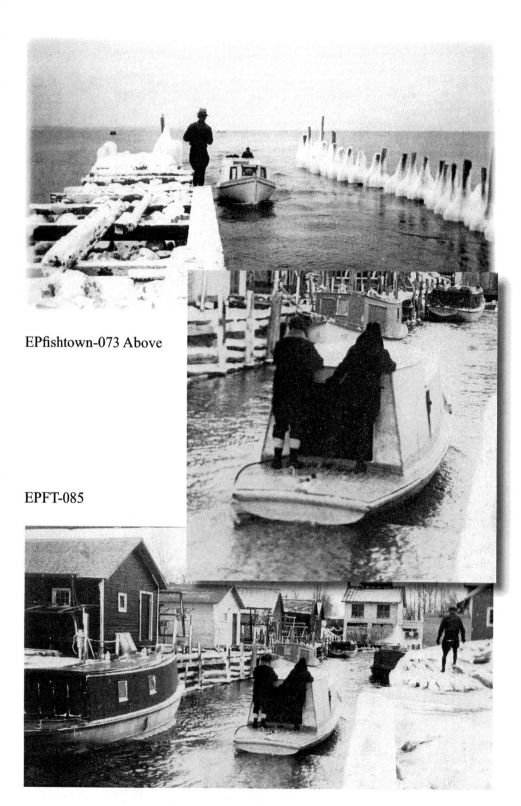

EPfishtown-073 Above

EPFT-085

EPFT-001 During the winter layover the fishermen were busy with repairing nets and getting ready for the spring fishing season and the annual ice harvest. In November 1928 notice was given to all fishermen that in the next year's season that the fish harvest must be stored in ice immediately after being caught.

Notice was given this early so that the fishermen would have ample time to put up the needed ice during their winter ice harvest for the following season.

EPFT-136

They would prepare often weeks in advance for the annual event of ice fishing or spearing in Leelanau Lake as well. They would prepare their coops and secure supplies of minnows in anticipation of the first cold snap that would allow them to venture out onto the ice to enjoy the sport.

EPfishtown-046 Above

EPleland-037 Above

EPleland-040 Below Tracey Grosvenor and John Van Raalte take a moment to smile for Erhardt's camera. John seems to have that "whats that crazy kid doing out here taking pictures of us?" look about him.

EPfishtown-043 Above Fish Tugs on Parade The Irene and the Fern-L Mail boat head up a lineup of famous Leland Fish Tugs in the Leland Harbor.

EPfishtown-097 Below The Teal has seen better days

EPleland-007 Above Hungry Gulls looking for a free meal outside Leland Harbor  EPleland-013 middle: Eeny meeny miney moe which gull has the tallest pole? Maybe this is just a gulls version of King of the Mountain. EPLeland-043 Bottom

EPleland-016 Looks like a November storm brewing and gaining steam to give the docks and beach a sound lashing

EPleland-019 Erhardt and company on a river outing

EPleland-022 Below

EPleland-025 Above this group appears to be on an outing to North Manitou Island to have their portrait taken next to the Giant Cherry Tree. Edmund Peters is at the far left.

EPleland-028 At the Bluffs south of Leland Arnold Peters is on the middle left of the photo.

EPFT-070

EPFT-040 Below

EPFT-049 Above Fish Tug Wolverine. Above Oscar Price and the Wolverine heading out to pull the nets that would hopefully fill the tug with a nice catch of Lake Trout or Chubs.

According to the Leelanau Enterprise the Wolverine was lost due to a fire that erupted from a leaky carburetor and quickly engulfed the interior of the Wolverine. It was only by chance that the Helen S was nearby and was able to reach Oscar Price and his son quickly. The Wolverine was taken in tow and after burning to the waterline sunk just outside the Leland Harbor entrance.

All efforts to raise it by the lifesaving crew from Manitou were in vain and the vessel was declared a total loss.
EPFT-082

EPFT-190 Helen S towing the Wolverine just prior to the Wolverine sinking outside of the harbor.
Shown to the right is the bell on the back of the Helen S. so named by Henry Steffens after his daughter.
EPfishtown-088 Below The Irene, Sambo, Helen S

EPFT-091 Above

EPFT-312

EPFT-094 Below

EPleland-046 There are a few views in this book of postcards that may not have been of Erhardt's work but were present in his collection, such as the one above.
You have to rely on the comparison of his handwriting on the negatives.

EPleland-049 Compare some of these photographs to Leland of today and I think you will agree that there has been a lot of change in the past 70 years.

EPleland-052

EPleland-276
Nicholas Hotel

EPleland-055

EPleland-058

EPleland-034 looking across the commons at Leland toward Roundtop.

EPleland-275
The Leland Enterprise Office as seen February 22nd 1926.

EPleland-061 Top Riverside Inn

EPleland-070 Middle

EPleland-085 Below

EPleland-064


EPleland-067 Below

EPleland-073 During those times when the weather did not cooperate and provide the snow needed for the horse drawn sleds cord wood was brought into town by truck.

EPleland-076 Below

EPleland-079

EPleland-094

EPleland-097

EPleland-106

EPleland-082

EPleland-244 The Leland Mercantile owned by Emil Pederson.

EPleland-247 Showing off for the boys

EPleland-248 and the boys.

EPFT-301 bottom
EPFT-145 Top

EPFT-302 South Manitou mailboat

EPFT-175 above The **Irene was owned by William Buckler and he was assisted by his sons Roy and George. The Irene was launched in October 1926.** The boat was 34 feet long and powered by a 4 cylinder Hines engine

The Irene is shown here being pulled up on shore most likely for repairs. EPFT-178 Leland petitioned for years to have improvements made at the creek so that they would have a safe haven harbor.

EPFT-223 Etta

EPFT-232

EPFT-199
EPFT-217 Opposite page

EPFT-208
EPFT-211
EPFT-214

EPfishtown-136 Above

EPFT-196 The COON, The WHY NOT Will H. purchased The Why Not in 1926 after George Cook received the SAMBO. Will Harting had retired but only took one summer off from fishing and spent the winter as a landlubber in Florida.

In the past Will Harting had been Oscar Price's partner. The Why Not was finally sold to Standar Motor Company.

EPFT-205 The Manitou and other boats are crowding the docks. The buildings were built by the fishermen to meet their needs and consisted of buildings for the nets, smokehouses, and icehouses. Many of the existing buildings are being used for gift shops.

EPFT-151
The Diamond

EPFT-154 Irene, Nu Deal and others pulled up for the winter.

EPFT-130a

EPFT-130 The seagull cafe, otherwise known as the Helen S is just around the corner from the Bluebird and is now open for business.

The Helen S was named after Henry Steffens daughter.

EPFT-202 The Helen S, Etta and others are enjoying a busy summer day at the docks. Leland has long been the summer home of many families who would travel from all points to spend careless summer days as resorters.

Many families have decades long histories of making Leland their summer home.

INSET In July of 1926 Two boys cruised Lake Michigan in a sailing canoe. HM Doolittle of Dallas Texas, and AW Canfield of Thomasville Texas along with their monkey mascot called Ingebor are sailing to Cheboygan where their family has a summer cottage.

EPFT-220 Above NU DEAL

The Life and Death of a Lumbering Town By Edmund Peters:

The lumber town of Good Harbor, on the shore of Good Harbor Bay on Lake Michigan is 7 miles south of Leland, in Leelanau County, came into being about 1875 with the building and sawmill by a man named Vine.

From the surrounding countryside he got white ash logs which he cut into 4 inch lumber for wagon tongues and shipped it by boat from his dock to Milwaukee and Chicago. His mill was a poor one and he was a poor business man and hard to work for.

After 2 years of operation Vine sold everything to Henry Schomberg of Milwaukee and Jake Scwartz of Leland who turned to making barrel Staves, headings and hoops, to supply the growing need for shipping pork, apples, fish and other products of the lakes region.

Before this time beginning perhaps about 1860 the firm of Fayette and Thiess built a dock on Good Harbor Bay about 2 miles west of where the town of Good Harbor later stood. Over this dock went propeller wood for the lake steamers, and lumber and lath from their mill, in which my grandfather Johann [John] Peters was an engineer.

One of the partners Isaac Pheat had been commodore of a fleet of 28 freight boats that ran between Chicago and Buffalo. Wood and logs were cut largely between Lime and Traverse lakes, taken across Traverse lake on scows pulled along a cable, stretched from shore to shore by two men , one at each end of the scow. A tramway extended from the shore of Traverse Lake to the company dock on Lake Michigan. This business lasted to about 1870.

Shortly after 1880 Schomberg bought out Schwartz's interests and built a big sawmill which had a capacity of 30,000 feet output in a 10 hour day, at about this time T.D. Wilce later of Empire organized the Lime Lake lumber company, built a 3 mile long plank road from Lime Lake to Good Harbor and over it hauled his lumber to the Schomberg dock. My father had his first experience as a lumberjack working for this company which lasted 8 years.

After 4 years of business Henry Schomberg sold his mill and docks to his brothers Richard and Henry who organized the Schomberg Hardwood Lumber Company of Good Harbor and expanded the business.

The boarding house at Good Harbor circa 1924 Below the Company store in the process of having the old shingles removed while being torn down by John Peters.

They cut and sold over their dock, lumber, cordwood, cedar ties, and Hemlock Bark, the latter used in tanning leather. They shipped mainly to Chicago and Milwaukee. Richard managed the business at Good Harbor and Otto stayed in Milwaukee, handling the sale of their products, and acting as buyer for mill supplies, stock for their stores at Good Harbor etc.

During the following years a small town grew up at Good Harbor, almost entirely owned by Schomberg Brothers. The dock was enlarged to a length of 500 feet, at which 4 schooners could be loaded at the same time. From this dock was shipped potatoes and other produce from the surrounding countryside, as well as the forest products.

The Dickey House

In 1894 the Schomberg Brothers built a dam on the small creek at Good Harbor, and built a cheese factory, using milk from the nearby farmers. The venture was not successful, however and after a year of operation was abandoned.

The Schomberg lumber company operated a hotel, two stores which became a shopping center for the farmers of the area, and a saloon without which no community was complete.

Like all towns Good Harbor had it's roughnecks and rough times. The township line between Centerville and Cleveland Townships ran down the middle of the main street of Good Harbor.

Centerville Township did not allow saloons, so Good Harbor's saloon was built on the Cleveland Township side of the street. Dan Buss presided as bartender.

When Richard Schomberg married in 1897, he provided 2 barrels of beer and a quantity of whiskey for the boys at the saloon. After imbibing freely of the free spirits the grateful boys became involved in brawls which nearly wrecked the saloon and furnishings, and Dan Buss resigned as bartender.

When Mr. Schomberg returned from his honeymoon, he brought with him an ex-pugilist named Billy Bites, a rather small man, and installed him as bartender.

On one occasion after that three lumber jacks, John Basch, Francis Duperron, and one Red Harp after an evening of imbibing and card playing refused to pay for their refreshments, and proceeded to get tough. Billy Bites went into action, which ended with the 3 laid out on the floor, willing and eager to pay. The new bartender had little trouble after that.

The Schombergs had what was then a novel idea for attracting business to their stores. Otto the buyer bought bankrupt and fire sale stocks of merchandise which were given as premiums and business prospered. At one time the store gave a pair of shoes for every 5.00 in trade, at another time a lady's hat with every $2.00 in purchases. At this time they employed a milliner to trim the hats to suit the customer

At a later time Otto purchased stick candy by the ton, a pound of which was given with each 1.00 purchase. As a child I was treated to this stick candy by my grandmother.

At one time Otto Schomberg procured 500 barrels of salt pork which they sold for 5.00 a 200 pound barrel. Three thousand derby hats were also given away in the store, a hat with each 5.00 purchase. Until a few years ago one could see farmers of Centerville and Cleveland Townships wearing derby hats in the fields.

The Schomberg Lumber Co. acquired several sections of timber in Kasson Township, south of Maple City, built and operated camps and hauled the logs to their mill in winter over a 14 mile long road which they built.

The road was kept iced by crews that worked at night. Logs were hauled on sleighs with 8 foot wide bunks loaded with 3,000 feet or more of logs.

They also bought logs from the farmers of Centerville and Cleveland townships, either on the stump or hauled to the mill by the farmers.

Usually only mature trees were cut and much of the area in which they did business is still well timbered and producing logs.

Richard Schomberg acquired a reputation and fair dealing among the farmers with whom he did business. He was want to tell his buyers "Give the farmer what he has coming and give Dick Schomberg what he has coming".

On more then one occasion a buyer found himself without a job when he was found to have cheated the farmer when scaling his logs. My father [John Peters] worked for the Schomberg Lumber company in 1896-98 as outside foreman buying logs and cordwood, scaling logs, keeping time, supervising the loading of schooners and looking after the tote road to Maple City.

His salary was $50.00 per month and board. Dock workers received 5 cents an hour and men stowing lumber in the holds of ships were paid 50 cents an hour as it required skill to pile lumber so it would not shift in rough weather.

Main Street of Good Harbor and the Saloon on the opposite page. Vessels were loaded largely by farmers who were called to work when the ships docked.

Schooners carried 75,000 to 100,000 feet of lumber, depending on the size of the vessel. At times there would be several vessels at dock waiting to be loaded.

Good Harbor had no protection from Northwest storms which are most prevalent on Lake Michigan, so vessels often had to leave dock and run for the protection of Manitou Islands. Sometimes storms arose too suddenly for them to get into deep water and they were driven ashore.

At one time a schooner which had taken on half it's cargo of 12,000 bushels of potatoes was driven ashore and filled with water. The Tug Williams was called from Manistee and dredged a channel through which it was pulled to deep water. Many were not so fortunate. The shore of Good Harbor Bay still shows evidence of the fate of several of these ships.

At the time my father was employed at Good Harbor the mill worked night and day through the winter and through the day through the summer through August. As many as 75 teams of horses were kept busy, hauling logs to the mill, lumber to the docks and supplies to the camps.

The lumber company owned 15 teams and the rest were owned by and rented from farmers and others who worked for the company. At it's peak the mill cut 8 million feet of lumber a year. My father was often sent to estimate timber that as to be bought from farmers. On one occasion he was sent to the farm of August Kurtshalz who had a stand of Elm and maple.

He estimated it at 75,000 feet and the actual cut was 77,000 feet. One of the trees, a giant elm produced 11 twelve foot logs which scaled to 3,000 feet. The Butt log 6 feet in diameter was big to go through the door. Schomberg made an offer of 10.00 to Dan Buss if he would trim it down to the necessary size between sunrise and sunset, nothing if he failed. Buss earned and won the 10.00. Maple logs brought 5 and 6 dollars per thousand, basswood 8.00.

After 1900 the supply of timber gradually decreased and less lumber went over the dock at Good Harbor each year. About 1910 the mill burned to the ground, as well as about 1 million feet of lumber in the yard. The mill was not rebuilt, Schomberg Lumber Co. went out of business, and Good Harbor soon became a ghost town.

In 1924 my father bought most of the remaining buildings including the barn, hotel, stores, a dwelling and blacksmith shop for $475.00. He and my brothers and I tore them down and sold the lumber. There are few traces left of the existence of the once busy town of Good Harbor. There is a road to the lake which ends at the remains of the dock from which hundreds of ship loads of fine lumber moved to the growing cities of Chicago and Milwaukee.

EPFT-166

EPFT-181 BONNIE LASS Owned by John Maleski and built by Adolph Johnson launched November 28th 1935. This represented the 3rd boat built and launched during 1935 by Adolph Johnson.

EPFT-169

EPleland-103 Ice fields and bergs crowd into shore driven by the wind in this circa 1925 view of Lake Michigan outside of leland.

EPFM-027 This photo of the IRENE as the caption states was taken off Leland in April.

EPFM-028

EPFT-187 Left

EPFT-268 Above  EPFT-193 Opposite page
EPFT-289 Diamond and Etta Below
**DIAMOND: William Carlson was the Owner.** In August 1941 William Carlson and his son Lester were out near Fox Island to pull their nets when the gas line sprung a leak and ignited a fire. All efforts to extinguish it failed and an explosion resulted, both men donned life preservers and jumped into the water, watching helplessly as their boat burned to the water line.

They attempted to make for one of the islands but in their weakened condition could not make shore. William Carlson passed away about 3 PM in the afternoon and his son Lester was located about 3AM the next morning by another fishing tug. He had spent nearly 20 hours in the water and suffered from severe burns and exposure.

EPleland-202 top

EPleland-199 left

EPleland-271 middle

EPleland-205 bottom

EPFT-226 Old Mother nature gives fishtown a good dusting and a hint of whats yet to come. The fishboats are still tied to their docks in readiness for the next days trip out to the lake to set or pull a few more nets before being laid up for the winter.

EPFT-229 The Helen S and Irene are set in direct contrast to the winter scene above on a much warmer and brighter day in Fishtown.

EPFT-235 Above

EPFT-238 Right Irene and

EPFT-241

EPFT-241 Left

EPFT-244 Above Nu Deal

EPFT-253 Below Pond boats

EPFT-256 Irene Sambo and Diamond

EPFT-265 JANICE A.

EPFT-250 IRENE

EPleland-272

EPleland-124

EPleland-121 The sawmill on Lake Leelanau

EPleland-127 Cottage under the Pines, this cottage sits to the South East of the Peters home in Leland.

EPleland-100 opposite page

EPleland-273 above

EPleland-112

EPleland-109 opposite page

EPleland-172

EPleland-187

EPleland-130 Skating as well as ice fishing were popular winter pastimes during an era where there was no Television or cable, video games or arcades. It was a time of community, social outings and simpler pleasures. Groups of Leland's youth out for a skate circa 1926

EPleland-133 In the bottom photo we have Erhardt and Wilfred Peters in the middle of the group and Marie and Charlotte Stephens along with Dorothy Schmidt standing together to Wilfred's right.

EPleland-270

EPleland-136

EPleland-139

EPleland-148

EPleland-154

EPleland-151

EPleland-255 opposite

Each year the fishermen would take part in the annual ice harvest in order to secure the amounts of ice they would need during the warmer days of summer to keep the fish from spoiling. Once the ice conditions were good, and a cold snap had hopefully creating a layer of ice about 12 inches deep the fishermen went to work.

They would plow the snow and mark the ice, cut it, and in 1931 had the use of a machine owned and operated by Edward Wichern to cut through most of the ice leaving a thin layer to be broken loose by a ice spud.

The blocks of ice weighing about 175 pounds would then be lifted onto sleighs. In the event that a truck was used it took 2 men to lift the ice up onto the truck because of the height of the truck bed. Trucks were used in 1921 and not again until 1931.

Sleighs were lower to the ground were preferred over trucks. They could hold more then the 25 cakes that could be placed on a truck as well. During the 1927 season workers put up 15,000 cakes of ice in the Mercantile Icehouse, 2,500 cakes per day over a 6 day period of harvesting.

Edward Wichern did the marking, Henry Steffens the sawing and splitting, Will Harting, Fred Anderson Jr. Gordon Carlson, and Roy Buckler as loaders complete the Lake crew, there were 4 teams hauling ice.

Source: Leelanau Enterprise:

EPleland-190 Moving a building across Lake Leelanau, I wonder how thick the ice would have to be in order to support the weight of 2 trucks and the building? Do any of the readers know the story behind this view?

EPleland-193 Cottages all boarded up for the season awaiting a fresh breath of spring to harken the arrival of the summer residents and turn this slumbering haven into a bustling scene of city weary travelers relaxing and enjoying their holiday up north.

EPleland-196 opposite page No snow plow here! pass the blanket!

EPleland-142

EPleland-145  The roads in and around leland in the 1920's were at times difficult to travel.  When you take a look at their condition it's not hard to appreciate how happy the locals were when the construction of the "Concrete Road" began.  A full series of pictures of the new road construction will appear in Refelctions of Leland.

EPleland-163 above

Bringing in the harvest, take a close look at the vintage tractor with it's steel wheels.

EPleland-166 Below

EPleland-118 A hard days work in the cherry orchard.

EPleland-175 opposite page 2 youngsters show off their buckets of cherries, one has to wonder how many went in the bucket, one for the bucket and 2 for me, yum!

EPleland-269 Cherry Co-operative.

EPleland-169

Charlie Kropp at his forge in Good Harbor. Photographs are numbered in order to make it easier to identify those that you might wish to order prints of. A link to the online album where you can easily order prints is available off from the http://blackcreekpress.com site. Prices start at 1.29 for a 4x6 print. It's my intent to make Erhardt's prints available, affordable, and accessible.

EPleland-252 Opposite Page

EPleland-178

EPleland-160 opposite page

EPleland-274 John Haeft and Erhardt Peters sawing logs. Photographer unknown.

EPFM-016 Captain George Cook tends to the never ending job of repairing the nets.

EPFT-344 Top Power house.

EPleland-251 A very old image copied from Erhardt's vintage collection.

EPFM-009

EPFM-014 Right

EPFM-015

EPFM-006 Above

EPFM-002 Right

EPFT-259

EPFT-274

EPFT-271

EPFT-277 Fisherman's Shack down the beach from Leland

EPFT-280 Old Docks

EPFT-262 Fish Tug Violet

EPFT-283

EPFT-286
EPFM-001 Opposite Oscar Price with his 39 pound 48 inch Lake Trout.

EPFM-003 Top
EPFM-005 Right
EPFM-007 Bottom

EPFM-010 Captain George Cook setting nets from the tug "Why Not"

EPFM-011 Lifting the nets on the Tug "Why Not" George was often assisted by Arthur McCarthy.

EPFM-025 Roy Buckler is in the dark coat and hat in these two photos on the bottom of the page.

EPFM-018 When the chub harvest was good, a catch might weigh in at 6 or 700 pounds. EPFM-020 at these times a 3rd man was added to the crew to help lift nets

EPFM-024 When the commercial fishing season was in full swing Trout, Chubs and Whitefish were being sought out by the local fishing boats.

EPFM-021 Above
EPFM-017 Left

EPFM-013

EPFM-022 Henry Steffens working on his nets. EPleland-258 An artist at work painting fishtown. EPFT-297 bottom view

EPFM-029 Fishermen attempting to retrieve their nets. Put yourself on those boats for a moment and imagine spending the day out in the weather, and the cold of that early spring day.

EPFM-030

EPFM-031 Another view of an attempt to make it into the harbor through the drift ice that has blown in and blocked the harbor. They are running the boat up on the ice and the men are placing their weight on the bow of the boat and attempting to push through the ice.

EPFM-037

EPFM-038 above

EPFM-039 left Tracey Grosvenor and an unidentified passenger.

EPFM-040

EPFM-041

EPFM-042

NU DEAL Men have rushed out to assist the Nu-Deal in breaking through the ice so that they can get the ship into the safety of the creek and harbor at Leland.

EPFT-341

EPFT-322

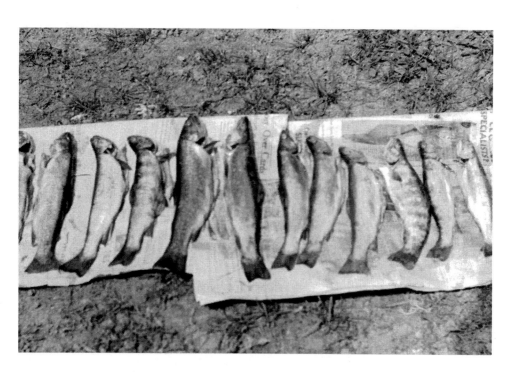

EPLH-002 North Manitou Island Lighthouse, notice the fog horn building starting to collapse into the Lake. The boilers and equipment were pulled out and a temporary shelter constructed over them in an attempt to save the equipment from being lost in Lake Michigan.

EPLH-068 A view from the top of the North Manitou Lighthouse.

EPLH-007 The North Manitou Lighthouse brick keepers quarters

EPLH-008

EPLH-061

EPLH-009 Opposite page Eventually all of these buildings were taken by erosion and collapsed.

EPLH-062

EPmanitou-003

EPmanitou-094 North Manitou Island Sunrise

EPLH-082

EPLH-076

EPmanitou-012 You can see the lighthouse out on the sandy point of North Manitou Island from near where an old wreck was laying in shallow water just off from the shore.

EPLH-089 North Manitou Crib Lighthouse under construction as seen from the Manitou Lightship. Construction of Concrete and Steel and currently sits in about 26 feet of water. The crib was floated out and filled once it was set upon it's location.

EPLH-014 Opposite page The crib Lighthouse was completed in the fall of 1934 but not put into service until the following spring of 1935.

EPLH-086 South Manitou Lighthouse was one of several built to provide safer travel along the Manitou Passage. The station was first established in 1839 and the current tower was first lit in 1872.

EPLS-007 North Manitou Island Coast Guard Station
EPLS-014
EPLS-017 Opposite page Fred Dustin on the Lifesaving station bell tower.

EPmanitou-001 Loads of apples or other items and supplies were towed from the island and mainland by the North Manitou.

EPmanitou-005 The Volunteer Rescue Boathouse 1854, Life saving Boat House 1877, Station Dwelling 1887, Hans Helseth House, Crew Ready Room 1895, and the Storm Tower and Flag Locker 1905 were the primary buildings at the complex on North Manitou Island.

EPmanitou-002

The beach in front of the North Manitou Coast Guard Station.

EPmanitou-004 middle

EPmanitou-003

EPmanitou-006 Tracy Grosevenor heading out from North Manitou Island.
EPmanitou-013 Left

EPmanitou-010 Below the Coast Guard Station complex dedicated as a National Historic Landmark in 1998

EPmanitou-007

EPmanitou-011

EPmanitou-009 Fern-L at the North Manitou Island Docks.

EPmanitou-037

EPmanitou-038

EPmanitou-039

EPmanitou-040

EPmanitou-048

EPmanitou-050 This is most likely the Docks on the west side of the island near Crescent.

EPmanitou-051

EPmanitou-064

EPmanitou-052

EPmanitou-053

EPmanitou-056

EPmanitou-015 Edwin Dalton the 19 year old son of John and Amanda Dalton died in 1880 and his grave north of the landing field was enclosed in a rustic wooden fence. Source: "Between Sunrise and Sunset"

EPmanitou-016 Opposite Page

These views of a grave site on North Manitou Island may or may not be that of Edwin Dalton. Any information that readers of this volume may have about this scene or that of the other gravesite that would help to establish their history would be greatly appreciated.

EPmanitou-020 The story was told that a Swedish ship sank in the bay and that the bodies of 6 or 7 men washed up on the North Manitou Island Shore and were buried there in sandy graves.

EPmanitou-019 Opposite Page and exposed skeleton

EPmanitou-035 Inset photo of Cemetery.

EPmanitou-017 below Human Bones

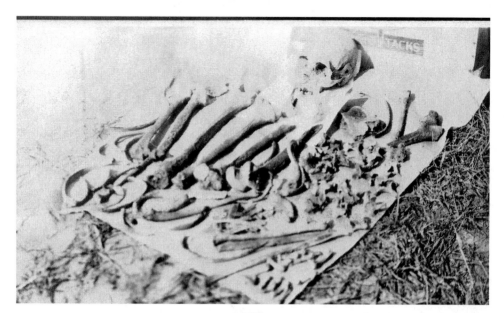

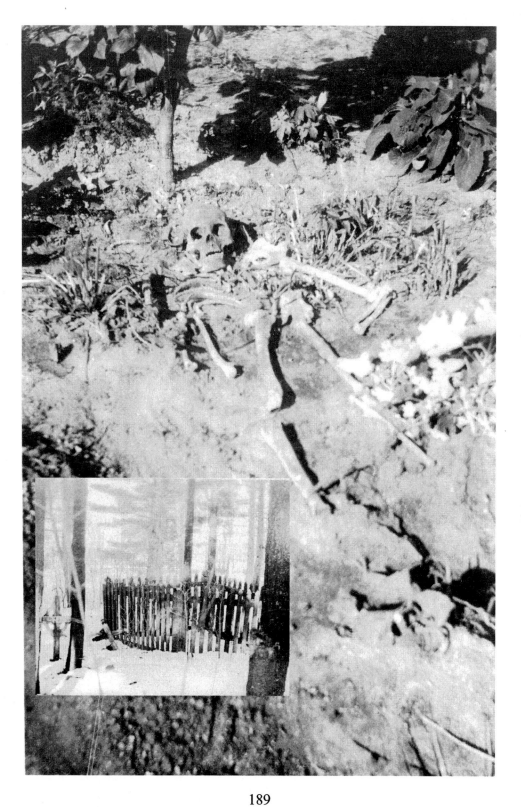

EPmanitou-026 Remnants of the Logging camps on North Manitou Island.

There was an active community on North Manitou Islands for many years. If you are interested in more information about life on North Manitou Island I would recommend "Between Sunrise and Sunset" by Rita Hadra Rusco.

EPmanitou-023 Left, a study of cabin construction.

EPmanitou-106 Our group has found their way to the Giant Cherry Tree, can you find Edmund Peters in this photograph?

EPLS-049 During the 1927 Season the Manitou Captain was George Navarre, John Peters had been transferred to Grays Reef to serve as Chief Engineer. LV-89 was constructed in 1908 in Muskegon Michigan at a cost of 37,500.00 and stationed at the Manitou Shoals from 1927 to 1933.

EPLS-050 Opposite page: There was always a lot of upkeep and maintenance aboard a lightship, the steam had to be kept up as well in the event that a fog rolled in and the fog horn was needed.
EPLS-052

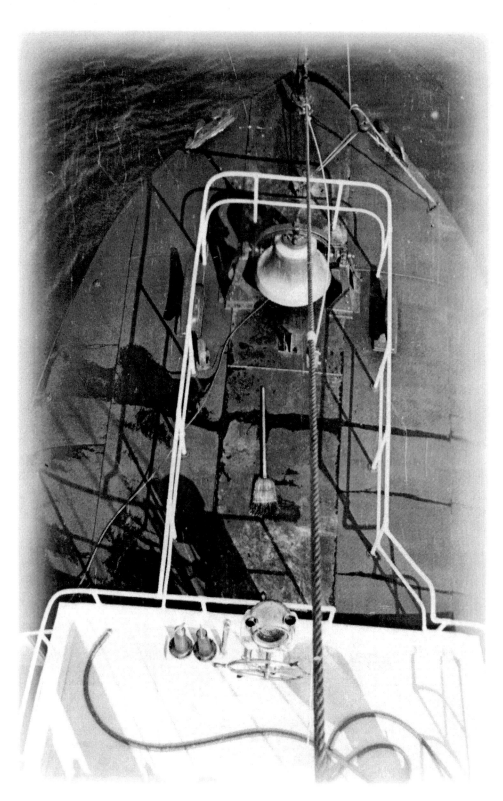

EPLS-009 Manitou Lightship tender boat above, this little vessel was carried atop LV-56 the last wooden Lightship on the Great Lakes.

EPLS-016 John Peters standing to the left of the Bell with Bert Benson on the deck of the lightship LV-56

EPLS-051 Left opposite page Looking down on the deck of the Manitou.

EPLS-056 John Peters and his wife Anna at the Leland home

EPLS-047 LV-103 built in 1920 was stationed at North Manitou Shoals from 1933 to 1934 before serving one year as a relief ship. LV-103 was then transferred to the Huron Station in Michigan where she served out her remaining years. In 1970 the Huron was donated to the City of Port Huron and is permanently on display as a Lightship Museum.

EPLS-048

EPLS-058 Above

EPLS- John Peters Chief Engineer of the Manitou Lightship and his brother Dick at the home in Leland.

EPLS-058

EPleland-088 I've always been a great fan of a good sunset and I think that this view makes for a great closing photograph to this first edition of Loving Leland. I hope you have enjoyed this journey as much as I have and I welcome comments, corrections or additional information about Leland, it's people, the fishing fleets and it's history.

This is not meant to be a comprehensive history of Leland but rather a showcase of the photographic works of Erhardt Peters.

I would be interested in gathering more in depth information of the Fishing fleet and fishing families of Leland, Manitou Island, the Lighthouse and it's keepers and the Manitou Lightship for future editions of Loving Leland.

I think that each of those 4 topics could warrant the creation of a separate book and that if the material in the form of photographs, postcards, and historical documents were made available I would be happy to assemble them into book form.

The most interesting material is always in private hands, family albums and that old shoebox in the closet. If you would like to share your families history please feel free to contact me.

Thank you for your patronage.

Black Creek Press
David K Petersen
1960 W Conrad Rd
Ludington Mi. 49431
http://blackcreekpress.com
info@blackcreekpress.com

The following includes the projects scheduled for completion by Black Creek Press and tentative release dates. Black Creek Press publishes local history books and CD's.

Erhardt Peters Volume 1
Spirit of the Lakes PUBLISHED July 2004

Erhardt Peters Volume 2
Carferries of Ludington November 2004

Erhardt Peters Volume 3
Great Loves Great Lakes Great Ships of the Inland Seas March 2005

Erhardt Peters Volume 4
Living Large on the Lower Lakers June 2005

Erhardt Peters Volume 5
Loving Leland PUBLISHED November 2004

Erhardt Peters Volume 6
Reflections of Leland February 2005

Erhardt Peters Volume 7
Land of Delight May 2005

Collective works of Erhardt Peters
November 2005

Carferry men of the Great Lakes volume 1.
100 biographies illustrated with photographs and with stories taken from oral interviews conducted with carferry workers on the Great Lakes
Submissions for inclusion are being accepted

**Independent car ferry union of the Great Lakes 1939 to 1941**
A history of the Independent Union of Carferrymen it's beginnings, struggles and dissolution. Including information on members, and illustrated with 200 photographs

**Wanted:** Information about any listed members of the Independent carferry union: The list of known members will be published online at http://carferry.info

**Sesquicentennial Edition of The History of Mason County** 2 CD set containing biographies and other information on the history of Mason County
Release date 2005.

**History of Scottville: Michigan Release Date 2006**
Information, letters, photographs old newspapers, etc. are wanted for purchase or loan for inclusion in this book.

**History of Custer Michigan Release Date 2006**
Information, letters, photographs old newspapers, etc. are wanted for purchase or loan for inclusion in this book.

**History of Freesoil Michigan Release date 2006**
Information, letters, photographs old newspapers, etc. are wanted for purchase or loan for inclusion in this book.

**History of Fountain Michigan Release date 2006**
Information, letters, photographs old newspapers, etc. are wanted for purchase or loan for inclusion in this book.

**History of Ludington Michigan Release date 2006**
Information, letters, photographs old newspapers, etc. are wanted for purchase or loan for inclusion in this book.

Wanted Information about the Scottville Tigers, photographs, postcards of the Ludington Mariners, Scrapbooks, photographs, postcards from the Mason County area. Lifesaving, Coast Guard, Fishtown in Ludington, Town of Lincoln, Hamlin, Buttersville, Finn Town letters, photos memorabilia.

## WANTED TO BUY:

I am always looking to purchase the following items:

Photographs and photograph albums of any topic prior to 1960.

I am especially interested of course in albums that contain maritime themes or other themes such as Logging, CCC camps, vacations on the Great Lakes, Lighthouses, Lightships etc. that might be used in future publications. Pictures, slides, and viewmaster reels.

Postcards, Postcard Albums of any theme prior to 1950 but I am especially interested in real photo postcards. Buying from 1 to 20,000 cards at a time.

Books: particularly older books pre-1930. Single books or by the box full. I have a wide interest in different types of books from yearbooks, to old illustrated texts and local history books.

Plat maps, plat books,

Some of the Books may not be necessarily rare or valuable but may contain graphics, engravings or colored plates that I collect.

Magazines pre-1930 of all types sizes and styles.

Advertising items, particularly items from Mason, Manistee or Oceana Counties in Michigan.

Ephemera of all types. Scrapbooks, booklets, old newspapers, letters, war correspondence from any war.

Then there are the other things from marbles to stereoscope cards, old toys, victrolas, records, etc.

One of the things that has always concerned me is the amount of history that is eaten by the local landfill and the truly rare images and history that is forgotten in a shoebox in the back closet. If you have such treasures and would like to sell or allow me to make copies for future publications [with credit given] please contact me.

## Selected Bibliography

Between Sunrise and Sunset: 1992 Rita Hadra Rusco

Leelanau Enterprise

Leelanau Enterprise 7-15-26

Leelanau Enterprise 8-19-26

Leelanau Enterprise 9-3-26

Leelanau Enterprise 11-11-26

Leelanau Enterprise 1-6-27

Leelanau Enterprise 1-13-27

Leelanau Enterprise 5-26-27

Leelanau Enterprise 9-1-27

Leelanau Enterprise 12-22-27

Leelanau Enterprise 3-22-28

Leelanau Enterprise 4-19-28

Leelanau Enterprise 10-2-28

Leelanau Enterprise 2-19-31

Leelanau Enterprise 10-1-31

Leelanau Enterprise 11-3-32

Good Harbor The Life and Death of a Lumbering Town By Edmund Peters

[Shown with John Peters Lightship Service Hat] Photo by Betty Doerr

Dave Petersen is a native of Ludington Michigan enjoys local history and collects vintage photographs from all areas of the country as well as maritime related emphemera, books, Ludington area history and advertising.

Dave maintains a local history site on the internet at http://ludingtonmichigan.net, a local information site at http://ludington.biz as well as a site for selling local history books at http://blackcreekpress.com.

He left the human services field after 25 years and is currently working on a series of books. This work represents his second Publication.